SIMON & SCHUSTER BOOKS FOR YOUNG READERS
An imprint of Simon & Schuster Children's Publishing Division
1230 Avenue of the Americas
New York, NY 10020
Copyright © 1997 by Frances Lincoln Limited
All illustrations reproduced by courtesy of the Trustees, The National Gallery, London
First published in Great Britain in 1997 by Frances Lincoln Limited,
4 Torriano Mews, Torriano Avenue, London NW5 2RZ

First American edition 1997

Book design by Kate Leitch

The text of this book is set in Bembo and Poetica Chancery IV

Printed in Hong Kong

1 3 5 7 9 10 8 6 4 2

Library of Congress Cataloguing-in-Publication Data
Bible. N.T. English, Authorized, Selections, 1996.
Stories from the New Testament.
p. cm.
ISBN 0-689-81297-3
I. Title.
BS2261.S56 1996
225.5'2036-dc21
96-46558
CIP

STORIES FROM ✠ ✠

THE NEW TESTAMENT

WITH MASTERWORK PAINTINGS INSPIRED BY THE STORIES

Simon & Schuster Books for Young Readers

CONTENTS

FEAR NOT, MARY

God has chosen a virgin called Mary to be the mother of a son who will redeem all people.
He sends his angel Gabriel to visit Mary and tell her the news.

AND IN THE SIXTH MONTH the angel Gabriel was sent from God unto a city of Galilee, named Nazareth, to a virgin espoused to a man whose name was Joseph, of the house of David; and the virgin's name was Mary.

And the angel came in unto her, and said, "Hail, thou that art highly favored, the Lord is with thee: blessed art thou among women."

And when she saw him, she was troubled at his saying, and cast in her mind what manner of salutation this should be.

And the angel said unto her, "Fear not, Mary: for thou hast found favor with God. And, behold, thou shalt conceive in thy womb, and bring forth a son, and shalt call his name Jesus. He shall be great, and shall be called the Son of the Highest: and the Lord God shall give unto him the throne of his father David. And he shall reign over the house of Jacob forever; and of his kingdom there shall be no end."

Then said Mary unto the angel, "How shall this be, seeing I know not a man?"

And the angel answered and said unto her, "The Holy Ghost shall come upon thee, and the power of the Highest shall overshadow thee: therefore also that holy thing which shall be born of thee shall be called the Son of God. And, behold, thy cousin Elisabeth, she hath also conceived a son in her old age: and this is the sixth month with her, who was called barren. For with God nothing shall be impossible."

And Mary said, "Behold the handmaid of the Lord; be it unto me according to thy word." And the angel departed from her.

OPVS CARO
LI·CRIVELLI
VENETI

NO ROOM AT THE INN

Mary and Joseph live in Galilee, which is ruled by the Romans. The Roman Emperor wants everyone to pay a new tax, and the couple must travel to Bethlehem to pay it, even though Mary's baby is expected very soon.

AND IT CAME TO PASS in those days, that there went out a decree from Caesar Augustus, that all the world should be taxed. (And this taxing was first made when Cyrenius was governor of Syria.) And all went to be taxed, every one into his own city.

And Joseph also went up from Galilee, out of the city of Nazareth, into Judaea, unto the city of David, which is called Bethlehem; (because he was of the house and lineage of David) to be taxed with Mary his espoused wife, being great with child.

And so it was, that, while they were there, the days were accomplished that she should be delivered. And she brought forth her firstborn son, and wrapped him in swaddling clothes, and laid him in a manger; because there was no room for them in the inn.

And there were in the same country shepherds abiding in the field, keeping watch over their flock by night. And, lo, the angel of the Lord came upon them, and the glory of the Lord shone around about them: and they were sore afraid.

And the angel said unto them, "Fear not: for, behold, I bring you good tidings of great joy, which shall be to all people. For unto you is born this day in the city of David a Savior, which is Christ the Lord. And this shall be a sign unto you; ye shall find the babe wrapped in swaddling clothes, lying in a manger."

And suddenly there was with the angel a multitude of the heavenly host praising God, and saying, "Glory to God in the highest, and on earth peace, good will toward men."

And it came to pass, as the angels were gone away from them into heaven, the shepherds said one to another, "Let us now go even unto Bethlehem, and see this thing which is come to pass, which the Lord hath made known to us." And they came with haste, and found Mary, and Joseph, and the babe lying in a manger.

And when they had seen it, they made known abroad the saying which was told them concerning this child. And all they that heard it wondered at those things which were told them by the shepherds. But Mary kept all these things, and pondered them in her heart.

THE STAR IN THE EAST

Herod, king of Judaea, is alarmed when he hears of the birth of a child who, the prophets claim, will grow up to be king.

NOW WHEN JESUS WAS BORN in Bethlehem of Judaea in the days of Herod the king, behold, there came wise men from the east to Jerusalem, saying, "Where is he that is born King of the Jews? For we have seen his star in the east, and are come to worship him."

When Herod the king had heard these things, he was troubled, and all Jerusalem with him. And when he had gathered all the chief priests and scribes of the people together, he demanded of them where Christ should be born. And they said unto him, "In Bethlehem of Judaea: for thus it is written by the prophet and thou Bethlehem, in the land of Juda, art not the least among the princes of Juda: for out of thee shall come a Governor, that shall rule my people Israel."

Then Herod, when he had privily called the wise men, enquired of them diligently what time the star appeared. And he sent them to Bethlehem, and said, "Go and search diligently for the young child; and when ye have found him, bring me word again, that I may come and worship him also."

When they had heard the king, they departed; and, lo, the star, which they saw in the east, went before them, till it stood over where the young child was.

When they saw the star, they rejoiced with exceeding great joy. And when they were come into the house, they saw the young child with Mary his mother, and fell down, and worshipped him: and when they had opened their treasures, they presented unto him gifts; gold, and frankincense, and myrrh.

And being warned of God in a dream that they should not return to Herod, they departed into their own country another way.

And when they were departed, behold, the angel of the Lord appeareth to Joseph in a dream, saying, "Arise, and take the young child and his mother, and flee into Egypt, and be thou there until I bring thee word: for Herod will seek the young child to destroy him."

When he arose, he took the young child and his mother by night, and departed into Egypt and was there until the death of Herod: that it might be fulfilled which was spoken of the Lord by the prophet, saying, "Out of Egypt have I called my son."

But when Herod was dead, behold, an angel of the Lord appeareth in a dream to Joseph in Egypt, saying, "Arise, and take the young child and his mother, and go into the land of Israel: for they are dead which sought the young child's life."

✠ SAINT MATTHEW 2 ✠

A VOICE IN THE WILDERNESS

As a young man, Jesus leaves Nazareth to travel to Jordan where his cousin, John the Baptist, is preaching a powerful message of repentance from the Old Testament.

IN THOSE DAYS came John the Baptist, preaching in the wilderness of Judaea, and saying, "Repent ye: for the kingdom of heaven is at hand. For this is he that was spoken of by the prophet Esaias, saying, 'The voice of one crying in the wilderness, Prepare ye the way of the Lord, make his paths straight.'"

And the same John had his raiment of camel's hair, and a leathern girdle about his loins; and his meat was locusts and wild honey.

Then went out to him Jerusalem, and all Judaea, and all the region around about Jordan, and were baptized of him in Jordan, confessing their sins.

But when he saw many of the Pharisees and Sadducees come to his baptism, he said unto them, "O generation of vipers, who hath warned you to flee from the wrath to come? Bring forth therefore fruits meet for repentance: and think not to say within yourselves 'We have Abraham to our father'; for I say unto you, that God is able of these stones to raise up children unto Abraham. And now also the axe is laid unto the root of the trees: therefore every tree which bringeth not forth good fruit is hewn down, and cast into the fire.

I indeed baptize you with water unto repentance: but he that cometh after me is mightier than I, whose shoes I am not worthy to bear: he shall baptize you with the Holy Ghost, and with fire: whose fan is in his hand, and he will thoroughly purge his floor, and gather his wheat into the garner; but he will burn up the chaff with unquenchable fire."

Then cometh Jesus from Galilee unto John, to be baptized of him. But John forbade him, saying, "I have need to be baptized of thee, and comest thou to me?"

And Jesus answering said unto him, "Suffer it to be so now: for thus it becometh us to fulfill all righteousness." Then he suffered him.

And Jesus, when he was baptized, went up straightway out of the water: and, lo, the heavens were opened unto him, and he saw the Spirit of God descending like a dove, and lighting upon him.

And lo a voice from heaven, saying, "This is my beloved Son, in whom I am well pleased."

HEROD'S BIRTHDAY

When he dares to speak out against King Herod's marriage to Herodias, John the Baptist makes a powerful enemy.

HEROD HIMSELF SENT FORTH and laid hold upon John, and bound him in prison for Herodias' sake, his brother Philip's wife: for he had married her. For John had said unto Herod, "It is not lawful for thee to have thy brother's wife."

Therefore Herodias had a quarrel against him, and would have killed him; but she could not.

For Herod feared John, knowing that he was a just man and a holy man, and observed him; and when he heard him, he did many things, and heard him gladly.

And when a convenient day was come, that Herod on his birthday made a supper to his lords, high captains, and chief estates of Galilee.

And when the daughter of the said Herodias came in, and danced, and pleased Herod and them that sat with him, the king said unto the damsel, "Ask of me whatsoever thou wilt, and I will give it thee." And he swore unto her, "Whatsoever thou shalt ask of me, I will give it thee, unto the half of my kingdom."

And she went, and said unto her mother, "What shall I ask?" And she said, "The head of John the Baptist."

And she came in straightway with haste unto the king, and asked, saying, "I will that thou give me by and by in a charger the head of John the Baptist."

And the king was exceeding sorry; yet for his oath's sake, and for their sakes which sat with him, he would not reject her.

And immediately the king sent an executioner, and commanded his head to be brought: and he went and beheaded him in the prison, and brought his head in a charger, and gave it to the damsel: and the damsel gave it to her mother.

And when his disciples heard of it, they came and took up his corpse, and laid it in a tomb.

A MARRIAGE IN CANA

*After Jesus is baptized, he begins to gather disciples around him. They are in Galilee for three days.
Some of the disciples go with Jesus and his mother to a wedding feast.*

AND THE THIRD DAY there was a marriage in Cana of Galilee; and the mother of Jesus was there: and both Jesus was called, and his disciples, to the marriage.

And when they wanted wine, the mother of Jesus saith unto him, "They have no wine."

Jesus saith unto her, "Woman, what have I to do with thee? Mine hour is not yet come."

His mother saith unto the servants, "Whatsoever he saith unto you, do it."

And there were set there six water pots of stone, after the manner of the purifying of the Jews, containing two or three firkins apiece.

Jesus saith unto them, "Fill the water pots with water." And they filled them up to the brim. And he saith unto them, "Draw out now, and bear unto the governor of the feast." And they bare it.

When the ruler of the feast had tasted the water that was made wine, and knew not whence it was: the governor of the feast called the bridegroom, and saith unto him, "Every man at the beginning doth set forth good wine; and when men have well drunk, then that which is worse: but thou hast kept the good wine until now."

This beginning of miracles did Jesus in Cana of Galilee, and manifested forth his glory; and his disciples believed in him.

After this he went down to Capernaum, he, and his mother, and his brethren, and his disciples: and they continued there not many days.

BY LAKE GENNESARET

*Jesus begins to preach in the synagogues. Because of the power of his teaching
and the miracles he performs, his fame soon spreads.*

AND IT CAME TO PASS, that, as the people pressed upon him to hear the word of God, he stood by the lake of Gennesaret and saw two ships standing by the lake: but the fishermen were gone out of them, and were washing their nets.

And he entered into one of the ships, which was Simon's, and prayed him that he would thrust out a little from the land. And he sat down, and taught the people out of the ship.

Now when he had left speaking, he said unto Simon, "Launch out into the deep, and let down your nets for a draught."

And Simon answering said unto him, "Master, we have toiled all the night, and have taken nothing: nevertheless at thy word I will let down the net."

And when they had this done, they enclosed a great multitude of fishes: and their net brake.

And they beckoned unto their partners in the other ship, that they should come and help them. And they filled both the ships, so that they began to sink.

When Simon Peter saw it, he fell down at Jesus' knees, saying, "Depart from me; for I am a sinful man, O Lord."

For he was astonished at the draught of the fishes which they had taken. And so was also James, and John, the sons of Zebedee, which were partners with Simon.

And Jesus said unto Simon, "Fear not; from henceforth thou shalt catch men."

And when they had brought their ships to land, they forsook all, and followed him.

ONLY BELIEVE

When they hear of the miracles Jesus works, crowds gather around him.
Even those in despair come, hoping to be healed by his touch.

AND, BEHOLD, there came a man named Jairus, and he was a ruler of the synagogue: and he fell down at Jesus' feet, and besought him that he would come into his house: for he had one only a daughter, about twelve years of age, and she lay dying. But as he went, the people thronged him.

And a woman having an issue of blood twelve years, which had spent all her living upon physicians, neither could be healed of any, came behind him, and touched the border of his garment: and immediately her issue of blood stanched.

And Jesus said, "Who touched me?" When all denied, Peter and they that were with him said, "Master, the multitude throng thee and press thee, and sayest thou, 'Who touched me?'"

And Jesus said, "Somebody hath touched me: for I perceive that virtue is gone out of me."

And the woman came trembling, and declared unto him before all the people for what cause she had touched him, and how she was healed immediately.

And he said unto her, "Daughter, be of good comfort: thy faith hath made thee whole; go in peace."

While he yet spake, there cometh one from the ruler of the synagogue's house, saying to him, "Thy daughter is dead; trouble not the Master."

But when Jesus heard it, he answered him, saying, "Fear not: believe only, and she shall be made whole."

And when he came into the house, he suffered no man to go in, save Peter, and James, and John, and the father and the mother of the maiden.

And all wept, and bewailed her: but he said, "Weep not; she is not dead, but sleepeth."

And they laughed him to scorn, knowing that she was dead.

And he put them all out, and took her by the hand, and called, saying, "Maid, arise."

And her spirit came again, and she arose straightway: and he commanded to give her meat.

And her parents were astonished: but he charged them that they should tell no man what was done.

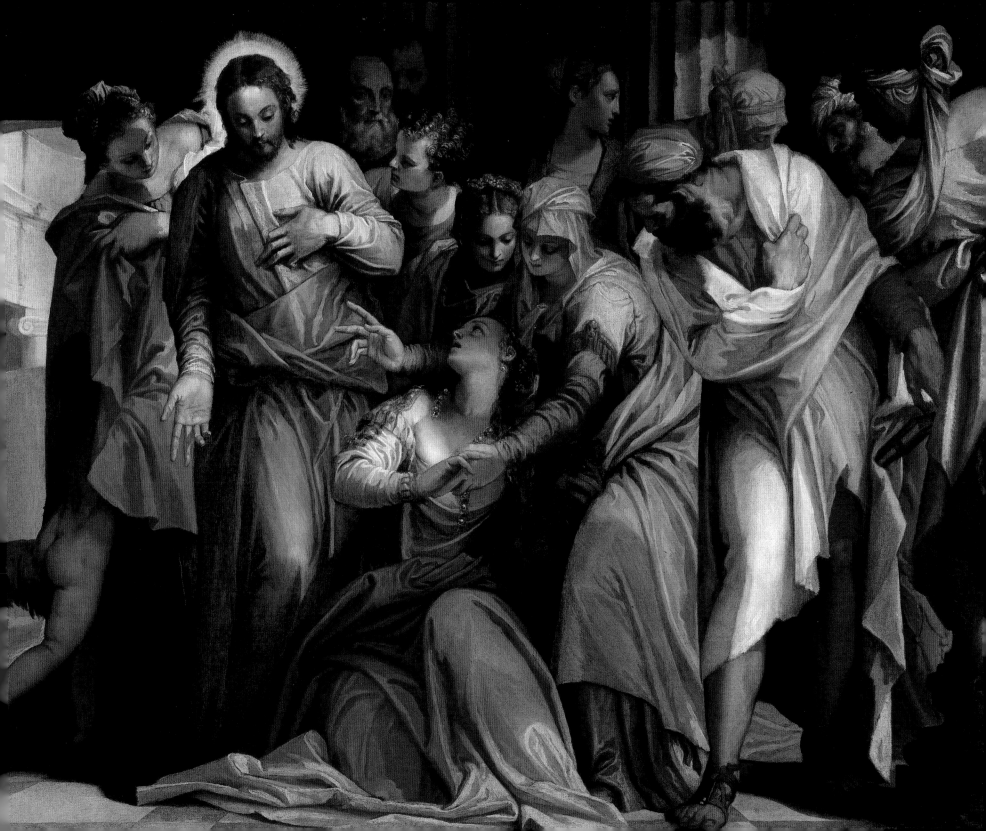

A MAN NAMED LAZARUS

Jesus leaves Judaea, but returns on hearing that Lazarus, the brother of Martha and Mary, is sick.
However, before Jesus reaches him, Lazarus is dead.

NOW BETHANY WAS NIGH unto Jerusalem. And many of the Jews came to Martha and Mary, to comfort them concerning their brother. Then Martha, as soon as she heard that Jesus was coming, went and met him: but Mary sat still in the house. Then said Martha unto Jesus, "Lord, if thou hadst been here, my brother had not died. But I know, that even now, whatsoever thou wilt ask of God, God will give it thee."

Jesus saith unto her, "Thy brother shall rise again."

Martha saith unto him, "I know that he shall rise again in the resurrection at the last day."

Jesus said unto her, "I am the resurrection, and the life: he that believeth in me, though he were dead, yet shall he live. And whosoever liveth and believeth in me shall never die. Believest thou this?"

She saith unto him, "Yea, Lord: I believe that thou art the Christ, the Son of God." And when she had so said, she went her way, and called Mary her sister, saying, "The Master is come, and calleth for thee."

Then when Mary was come where Jesus was, she fell down at his feet, saying unto him, "Lord, if thou hadst been here, my brother had not died."

When Jesus therefore saw her weeping, and the Jews also weeping which came with her, he groaned in the spirit, and was troubled, and said, "Where have ye laid him?" They said unto him, "Lord, come and see."

Jesus wept. Then said the Jews, "Behold how he loved him."

Jesus therefore again groaning in himself cometh to the grave. It was a cave, and a stone lay upon it.

Jesus said, "Take ye away the stone."

Martha saith unto him, "Lord, by this time he stinketh: for he hath been dead four days."

Jesus saith unto her, "Said I not unto thee, that, if thou wouldest believe, thou shouldest see the glory of God?"

Then they took away the stone from the place where the dead was laid. And Jesus lifted up his eyes, and said, "Father, I thank thee that thou hast heard me. And I knew that thou hearest me always: but because of the people which stand by I said it, that they may believe that thou hast sent me." And he cried with a loud voice, "Lazarus, come forth."

And he that was dead came forth, bound hand and foot with graveclothes: and his face was bound about with a napkin.

Then many of the Jews which had seen the things which Jesus did, believed in him. But some of them went their ways to the Pharisees, and told them what things Jesus had done.

THE LAST SUPPER

*By his teaching, Jesus has made many enemies. Knowing that time is short, he takes a last supper
with his disciples to celebrate the feast of the Passover.*

AND AS THEY WERE EATING, Jesus took bread, and blessed it, and brake it, and gave it to the disciples, and said, "Take, eat; this is my body."

And he took the cup, and gave thanks, and gave it to them, saying, "Drink ye all of it; for this is my blood of the new testament, which is shed for many for the remission of sins. But I say unto you, I will not drink henceforth of this fruit of the vine, until that day when I drink it new with you in my Father's kingdom."

Jesus knowing that the Father had given all things into his hands, and he was come from God, and went to God; he riseth from supper, and laid aside his garments; and took a towel, and girded himself. After that he began to wash the disciples' feet, and to wipe them with the towel wherewith he was girded.

Then cometh he to Simon Peter: and Peter saith unto him, "Lord, dost thou wash my feet?"

Jesus answered and said unto him, "What I do thou knowest not now; but thou shalt know hereafter."

Peter saith unto him, "Thou shalt never wash my feet."

Jesus answered him, "If I wash thee not, thou hast no part with me."

Simon Peter saith unto him, "Lord, not my feet only, but also my hands and my head."

Jesus saith to him, "He that is washed needeth not save to wash his feet, but is clean every whit."

So after he had washed their feet, and had taken his garments, and was set down again, he said unto them, "Know ye what I have done to you? Ye call me Master and Lord: and ye say well; for so I am. If I then, your Lord and Master, have washed your feet; ye also ought to wash one another's feet. For I have given you an example, that ye should do as I have done to you."

When Jesus had thus said, he was troubled in spirit, and said, "Verily, verily, I say unto you, that one of you shall betray me."

Now there was lying on Jesus' bosom one of his disciples, whom Jesus loved. He then saith unto him, "Lord, who is it?"

Jesus answered, "He to whom I shall give a sop, when I have dipped it." And when he had dipped the sop, he gave it to Judas Iscariot, the son of Simon.

He then having received the sop went immediately out: and it was night.

SAINT MATTHEW 26,
SAINT JOHN 13

THE AGONY IN THE GARDEN

When the meal is over, Jesus goes with a few disciples to the garden of Gethsemane. While his exhausted disciples sleep,
he spends the night praying for strength to accept what lies before him.

THEN COMETH JESUS unto a place called Gethsemane, and saith unto the disciples, "Sit ye here, while I go and pray yonder."

And he took with him Peter and the two sons of Zebedee, and began to be sorrowful and very heavy.

Then saith he unto them, "My soul is exceeding sorrowful, even unto death: tarry ye here, and watch with me."

And he went a little further, and fell on his face, and prayed, saying, "O my Father, if it be possible, let this cup pass from me: nevertheless not as I will, but as thou wilt."

And he cometh unto the disciples, and findeth them asleep, and saith unto Peter, "What, could ye not watch with me one hour? Watch and pray, that ye enter not into temptation: the spirit is willing, but the flesh is weak."

He went away again the second time, and prayed, saying, "O my Father, if this cup may not pass away from me, except I drink it, thy will be done."

And he came and found them asleep again: for their eyes were heavy.

And he left them, and went away again, and prayed the third time, saying the same words.

Then cometh he to his disciples, and saith unto them, "Sleep on now, and take your rest: behold, the hour is at hand, and the Son of man is betrayed into the hands of sinners. Rise, let us be going: behold, he is at hand that doth betray me."

THE TRAITOR'S KISS

For a reward of thirty pieces of silver, Judas, one of the disciples, has agreed to betray Jesus to the chief priests and elders who are his enemies. Jesus knows what Judas intends, but chooses to go ahead with God's plan.

AND WHILE HE YET SPAKE, lo, Judas, one of the twelve, came, and with him a great multitude with swords and staves, from the chief priests and elders of the people.

Now he that betrayed him gave them a sign, saying, "Whomsoever I shall kiss, that same is he: hold him fast."

And forthwith he came to Jesus, and said, "Hail, master," and kissed him.

And Jesus said unto him, "Friend, wherefore art thou come?" Then came they, and laid hands on Jesus, and took him.

And, behold, one of them which were with Jesus stretched out his hand, and drew his sword, and struck a servant of the high priest's, and smote off his ear.

Then said Jesus unto him, "Put up again thy sword into his place: for all they that take the sword shall perish with the sword. Thinkest thou that I cannot now pray to my Father, and he shall presently give me more than twelve legions of angels? But how then shall the scriptures be fulfilled, that thus it must be?"

In that same hour said Jesus to the multitudes, "Are ye come out as against a thief with swords and staves for to take me? I sat daily with you teaching in the temple, and ye laid no hold on me." But all this was done, that the scriptures of the prophets might be fulfilled.

Then all the disciples forsook him, and fled.

And they that had laid hold on Jesus led him away to Caiaphas the high priest, where the scribes and the elders were assembled.

When the morning was come, all the chief priests and elders of the people took counsel against Jesus to put him to death: and when they had bound him, they led him away, and delivered him to Pontius Pilate the governor.

Then Judas, which had betrayed him, when he saw that he was condemned, repented himself, and brought again the thirty pieces of silver to the chief priests and elders, saying, "I have sinned in that I have betrayed the innocent blood." And they said, "What is that to us? See thou to that."

And he cast down the pieces of silver in the temple, and departed, and went and hanged himself.

SAINT MATTHEW
26 & 27

A CROWN OF THORNS

The chief priests and elders want Jesus crucified for claiming to be the Son of God.
Pontius Pilate believes Jesus is innocent, but he gives way to pressure and allows the crucifixion to go ahead.

AND THEY STRIPPED HIM, and put on him a scarlet robe. And when they had plaited a crown of thorns, they put it upon his head, and a reed in his right hand: and they bowed the knee before him, and mocked him, saying, "Hail, King of the Jews!"

And they spit upon him, and took the reed, and smote him on the head. And after that they had mocked him, they took the robe off from him, and put his own raiment on him, and led him away to crucify him.

And when they were come unto a place called Golgotha, that is to say, a place of a skull, they gave him vinegar to drink mingled with gall: and when he had tasted thereof, he would not drink.

And they crucified him, and parted his garments, casting lots. And sitting down they watched him there; and set up over his head his accusation written, THIS IS JESUS THE KING OF THE JEWS.

Then were there two thieves crucified with him, one on the right hand, and another on the left.

And they that passed by reviled him, wagging their heads, and saying, "Thou that destroyest the temple, and buildest it in three days, save thyself. If thou be the Son of God, come down from the cross."

Likewise also the chief priests mocking him, with the scribes and elders, said, "He saved others; himself he cannot save. If he be the King of Israel, let him now come down from the cross, and we will believe him."

Now from the sixth hour there was darkness over all the land. And about the ninth hour Jesus cried with a loud voice, saying, "*Eli, Eli, lama sabachthani?*" That is to say, "My God, my God, why hast thou forsaken me?"

Some of them that stood there, when they heard that, said, "This man calleth for Elias." And straightway one ran and took a sponge, and filled it with vinegar, and put it on a reed, and gave him to drink. The rest said, "Let us see whether Elias will come to save him."

Jesus, when he had cried again with a loud voice, yielded up the ghost.

And, behold, the veil of the temple was rent in twain from the top to the bottom; and the earth did quake, and the rocks rent; and the graves were opened; and many bodies of the saints which slept arose, and came out of the graves after his resurrection, and went into the holy city, and appeared unto many.

Now when the centurion, and they that were with him, watching Jesus, saw the earthquake, and those things that were done, they feared greatly, saying, "Truly this was the Son of God."

WOMAN, WHY WEEPEST THOU?

Pontius Pilate gives the disciples permission to take the body of Jesus away for burial.
They wrap it in linen, and lay it in a new sepulchre near the place where he was crucified.

THE FIRST DAY of the week cometh Mary Magdalene early, when it was yet dark, unto the sepulchre, and seeth the stone taken away. Then she runneth, and cometh to Simon Peter, and to the other disciple, whom Jesus loved, and saith unto them, "They have taken away the Lord out of the sepulchre, and we know not where they have laid him."

Peter therefore went forth, and that other disciple, and came to the sepulchre. So they both ran together: and the other disciple did outrun Peter, and came first to the sepulchre. And he stooping down, and looking in, saw the linen clothes lying; yet went he not in.

Then cometh Simon Peter following him, and went into the sepulchre, and seeth the linen clothes lie, and the napkin that was about his head, not lying with the linen clothes, but wrapped together in place by itself.

Then went in also that other disciple, and he saw, and believed. For as yet they knew not the scripture, that he must rise again from the dead. Then the disciples went away unto their own home.

But Mary stood without at the sepulchre weeping: and as she wept, she stooped down, and looked into the sepulchre, and seeth two angels in white sitting, the one at the head, and the other at the feet, where the body of Jesus had lain.

And they say unto her, "Woman, why weepest thou?" She saith unto them, "Because they have taken away my Lord, and I know not where they have laid him." And when she had thus said, she turned herself back, and saw Jesus standing, and knew not that it was Jesus.

Jesus saith unto her, "Woman, why weepest thou? Whom seekest thou?"

She, supposing him to be the gardener, saith unto him, "Sir, if thou have borne him hence, tell me where thou hast laid him, and I will take him away."

Jesus saith unto her, "Mary." She turned herself, and saith unto him, "*Raboni*"; which is to say, "Master."

Jesus saith unto her, "Touch me not; for I am not yet ascended to my Father: but go to my brethren, and say unto them, I ascend unto my Father, and your Father; and to my God, and your God."

Mary Magdalene came and told the disciples that she had seen the Lord, and that he had spoken these things unto her.

 SAINT JOHN 20

MY LORD AND MY GOD

On the evening of the day he appeared to Mary Magdalene, Jesus appears again to a gathering of his disciples.

THEN THE SAME DAY at evening, being the first day of the week, when the doors were shut where the disciples were assembled for fear of the Jews, came Jesus and stood in the midst, and saith unto them, "Peace be unto you."

And when he had so said, he showed unto them his hands and his side. Then were the disciples glad, when they saw the Lord.

Then said Jesus to them again, "Peace be unto you: as my Father hath sent me, even so send I you." And when he had said this, he breathed on them, and saith unto them, "Receive ye the Holy Ghost: whosoever sins ye remit, they are remitted unto them; and whosoever sins ye retain, they are retained."

But Thomas, one of the twelve, called Didymus, was not with them when Jesus came.

The other disciples therefore said unto him, "We have seen the Lord." But he said unto them, "Except I shall see in his hands the print of the nails, and put my finger into the print of the nails, and thrust my hand into his side, I will not believe."

And after eight days again his disciples were within, and Thomas with them: then came Jesus, the doors being shut, and stood in the midst, and said, "Peace be unto you."

Then saith he to Thomas, "Reach hither thy finger, and behold my hands; and reach hither thy hand, and thrust it into my side: and be not faithless, but believing."

And Thomas answered and said unto him, "My Lord and my God."

Jesus saith unto him, "Thomas, because thou hast seen me, thou hast believed: blessed are they that have not seen, and yet have believed."

And many other signs truly did Jesus in the presence of his disciples, which are not written in this book: but these are written, that ye might believe that Jesus is the Christ, the Son of God; and that believing ye might have life through his name.

ABIDE WITH US

On the third day after the Crucifixion, two of the disciples set out on foot to a village not far from Jerusalem.

AND, BEHOLD, two of them went that day to a village called Emmaus, which was from Jerusalem about threescore furlongs. And they talked together of all these things which had happened.

And it came to pass, that, while they communed together and reasoned, Jesus himself drew near, and went with them. But their eyes were holden that they should not know him. And he said unto them, "What manner of communications are these that ye have one to another, as ye walk, and are sad?"

And the one of them, whose name was Cleopas, answering said unto him, "Art thou only a stranger in Jerusalem, and hast not known the things which are come to pass there in these days?"

And he said unto them, "What things?"

And they said unto him, "Concerning Jesus of Nazareth, which was a prophet mighty in deed and word before God and all the people: and how the chief priests and our rulers delivered him to be condemned to death, and have crucified him. But we trusted that it had been he which should have redeemed Israel: and beside all this, today is the third day since these things were done.

Yea, and certain women also of our company made us astonished, which were early at the sepulchre; and when they found not his body, they came, saying that they had also seen a vision of angels, which said that he was alive. And certain of them which were with us went to the sepulchre, and found it even so as the women had said: but him they saw not."

Then he said unto them, "O fools, and slow of heart to believe all that the prophets have spoken. Ought not Christ to have suffered these things, and to enter into his glory?" And beginning at Moses and all the prophets, he expounded unto them in all the scriptures the things concerning himself.

And they drew nigh unto the village, whither they went: and he made as though he would have gone further. But they constrained him, saying, "Abide with us: for it is toward evening, and the day is far spent." And he went in to tarry with them.

And it came to pass, as he sat at meat with them, he took bread, and blessed it, and brake, and gave to them.

And their eyes were opened, and they knew him; and he vanished out of their sight.

 SAINT LUKE 24

WHY PERSECUTEST THOU ME?

After Jesus ascends into heaven his followers risk death by spreading his message far and wide.
One of their fiercest enemies is a man called Saul.

AND AS SAUL JOURNEYED, he came near Damascus: and suddenly there shined around about him a light from heaven. And he fell to the earth, and heard a voice saying unto him, "Saul, Saul, why persecutest thou me?"

And he said, "Who art thou, Lord?" And the Lord said, "I am Jesus whom thou persecutest: it is hard for thee to kick against the pricks."

And he trembling and astonished said, "Lord, what wilt thou have me to do?" And the Lord said unto him, "Arise, and go into the city, and it shall be told thee what thou must do." And the men which journeyed with him stood speechless, hearing a voice, but seeing no man.

And Saul arose from the earth; and when his eyes were opened, he saw no man: but they led him by the hand, and brought him into Damascus. And he was three days without sight, and neither did eat or drink.

And there was a certain disciple at Damascus, named Ananias; and to him said the Lord in a vision, "Ananias." And he said, "Behold, I am here, Lord."

And the Lord said unto him, "Arise, and go into the street which is called Straight, and enquire in the house of Judas for one called Saul, of Tarsus: for, behold, he prayeth, and hath seen in a vision a man named Ananias coming in, and putting his hand on him, that he might receive his sight."

Then Ananias answered, "Lord, I have heard by many of this man, how much evil he hath done to thy saints at Jerusalem. And here he hath authority from the chief priests to bind all that call on thy name."

But the Lord said unto him, "Go thy way: for he is a chosen vessel unto me, to bear my name before the Gentiles, and kings, and the children of Israel. For I will show him how great things he must suffer for my name's sake."

And Ananias went his way, and entered into the house; and putting his hands on him said, "Brother Saul, the Lord, even Jesus, that appeared unto thee in the way as thou camest, hath sent me, that thou mightest receive thy sight, and be filled with the Holy Ghost."

And immediately there fell from his eyes as it had been scales: and he received sight forthwith, and arose, and was baptized.

Then was Saul certain days with the disciples which were at Damascus. And straightway he preached Christ in the synagogues, that he is the Son of God.

INDEX OF PAINTINGS

The Annunciation, with Saint Emidius (detail)
CARLO CRIVELLI
(*c.* 1430/5-1494)

Crivelli was born in Venice, but spent most of his life in eastern central Italy. He became famous as a painter of altarpieces, like this one depicting the Annunciation, which was painted for the church of S. Annunziata in Ascoli Piceno. Kneeling beside the angel Gabriel is Saint Emidius, Ascoli's patron saint, holding a model of the town.

The Adoration of the Shepherds (detail)
THE LE NAIN BROTHERS
Antoine (*c.* 1600-48), Louis (*c.* 1603-48)
and Mathieu (*c.* 1607-77)

These three artist brothers were born in Laon. Antoine entered the painters' guild of Saint Germain-des-Près, Paris, and established a studio in the city where the brothers worked together, mostly on portraits and scenes of peasant life. Here, both the animals and shepherds visiting the newly-born Jesus are depicted with affectionate detail.

The Baptism of Christ (detail)
AFTER PIETRO PERUGINO
(living 1469; d. 1523)

This is a copy of Perugino's *Baptism of Christ* (in Musée des Beaux-Arts, Rouen), which was painted by an unknown artist in the mid-19th century. Pietro Vanucci, known as Perugino, was named after the Italian town of Perugia, where he mainly worked. He was the most sought-after painter in Italy between 1490 and 1505, but his work was regarded as outmoded in his later years.

The Adoration of the Kings (detail)
SANDRO BOTTICELLI
(*c.* 1445-1510)

Botticelli was born in Florence and studied there under the painter and monk Fra Filippo Lippi, whose influence is evident in this early work. During his long and active career, he frequently worked for the Medici family, who ruled Florence, and the costumes shown here reflect the fashions worn at their court. Although Botticelli was famous in his day, his popularity today is largely due to the rediscovery of his work by the English Pre-Raphaelite painters of the 19th century.

Page 21
The Miraculous Draught of Fishes (detail)
Peter Paul RUBENS
(1577–1640)

One of the greatest artists of the 17th century, the Flemish painter Rubens was also a diplomat whose travels took him all over Europe. The influence of Italian Baroque style can be seen in this working drawing. The turbulent sea and sky, and the frenzied struggles of the fishermen as they strain to control the bursting net, form a dramatic contrast with the static figures of Christ and Saint Peter at the center of the composition.

Page 17
The Feast of Herod (detail)
GIOVANNI Di PAOLO
(active by 1417; d. 1482)

Giovanni di Paolo, sometimes known as Giovanni dal Poggio, was one of the most important painters in Siena during the early 15th century. He is best known for his strong sense of narrative, evident in lively altarpiece panels like this one, taken from a series of five scenes telling the story of Saint John the Baptist. On the left, Herod shrinks back in horror as the saint's severed head is presented to him on a dish, while on the right, Herodias' daughter Salome smiles at seeing her mother's wish fulfilled.

Page 19
The Marriage at Cana (detail)
MATTIA PRETI
(1613–99)

Preti was one of the chief painters working in Rome in the mid-17th century, after which he moved to Naples, becoming a leading artist there. He was greatly influenced by Venetian painters, especially Veronese. Preti painted The Marriage at Cana on several occasions during his years in Naples. From 1660 he lived in Malta, where he was active until his death.

Page 23
Christ Addressing a Kneeling Woman (detail)
Paolo VERONESE
(c. 1528–88)

Born in Verona, Paolo Caliari was later known as Veronese after his home town. In the late 1550s he moved to Venice, where he was heavily influenced by Titian and other Venetian painters. He became one of the leading painters of the late 16th century and, in turn, deeply influenced later artists such as Tiepolo and Delacroix. This early work typifies Veronese's love of grand composition and luminous color.

44

PAGE 25
The Raising of Lazarus (detail)
SEBASTIANO DEL PIOMBO
(*c.* 1485–1547)

Sebastiano was born and trained in Venice, probably with Giorgione, but later moved to Rome. In 1531 he was nominated to the office of the Piombo (keeper of the Papal Seal), hence his name. He was a friend of Michelangelo, who provided the design for this painting.

BACK COVER AND PAGE 27
Christ Washing His Disciples' Feet (detail)
JACOPO TINTORETTO
(1518–94)

The son of a dyer (*tintore*), Tintoretto was named after his father's occupation. For most of his life he lived and worked in Venice, where he came under the influence of Titian. He had a highly organized workshop dealing with varied commissions, from portraits to huge compositions. Tintoretto is best known for large religious paintings in which dramatic gestures and lighting are used to help tell a story.

PAGE 29
The Agony in the Garden (detail)
GIOVANNI BELLINI
(active *c.* 1459; d. 1516)

A leading painter in Venice, Bellini was one of the first great Italian painters to use oil paint. His early work shows influences from his brother-in-law, Mantegna, and this painting resembles a version of the same subject by him. Bellini is celebrated for the way he painted natural light, here the breaking light of dawn. A feeling of foreboding is emphasized by the eerie light and the stark landscape.

PAGE 31
The Betrayal of Christ (detail)
UGOLINO DI NERIO
(active 1317; d. 1339/49?)

Although he came from Siena, Ugolino did most of his important work in Florence. This painting is part of an altarpiece probably commissioned by the Alamanni family for the Florentine church of Santa Croce. Here, Judas identifies Christ with a kiss as the soldiers close in to arrest him. The artist's style suggests that he was taught by Duccio.

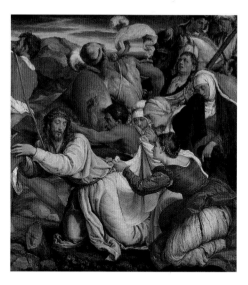

PAGE 33
The Way to Calvary (detail)
JACOPO BASSANO
(active *c.* 1535; d. 1592)

Jacopo dal Ponte belonged to a family of painters from Bassano, near Venice, hence his name. He worked there throughout his life and by 1545 he was the leading painter in his region. Here he paints Christ, collapsed under the weight of his cross. Saint Veronica rushes forward, offering him a cloth to wipe himself. Miraculously, an impression of his face is left on it.

PAGE 35
Noli me Tangere (detail)
TITIAN
(active *c.* 1506; d.1576)

The Venetian painter, Titian, is one of the most important and influential figures in the history of art, best known for his free brush style and use of color. In this early painting, the dramatic moment when Mary Magdalene recognizes Christ is emphasized by the form of the landscape—the shapes of the tree and bush echo the poses of the figures.

PAGE 37
The Incredulity of Saint Thomas (detail)
GUERCINO
(1591–1666)

The Bolognese painter Giovanni Francesco Barbieri, called Guercino (the "squint-eyed"), is known for his horizontal compositions with half-length figures that give a dramatic effect. The Carracci, Caravaggio, and the Venetian School were important influences on his work. *The Incredulity of Saint Thomas* was painted for Bartolomeo Fabri, who lived in Cento, Guercino's hometown.

PAGE 39
The Supper at Emmaus (detail)
MICHELANGELO MERISI DA CARAVAGGIO
(1571–1610)

The artist was probably born in Milan. Famous for his startling compositions and impressive use of light and shade, Caravaggio loved to paint dramatic subjects that could do justice to his style. Here the viewer is invited to sit at the table, just as the disciples recognize Christ. Caravaggio fled to Naples in 1606 having killed a man in a duel, and he died on his way back to Rome several years later.

PAGE 41
The Conversion of Saint Paul (detail)
UNKNOWN ARTIST, ITALIAN, FERRARESE

The unknown painter of this work came from Ferrara, an important Italian city that maintained a strong local painting tradition throughout the 15th and 16th centuries. Flung to the ground by the blinding light, Saint Paul hides his face from the dazzling vision of Christ that appears out of a cloud in the upper right-hand corner.